TIME WILL TELL

TIME WILL TELL

poems and profiles
DORIS ABRAMSON

Haley's

Athol, Massachusetts

Haley's
Post Office Box 248
Athol, Massachusetts 01331
1.800.215.8805 • haley.antique@verizon.net
www.haleysantiques.com

With thanks to Mary-Ann DeVita Palmieri and bg Thurston.

ACKNOWLEDGMENTS:

Grateful acknowledgment is made to the following publications:
University of Massachusetts, Amherst, Massachusetts, *The Massachusetts Review,* XXIII, No. 3, "A Tribute to Denis Johnston," pp. 389-409, 1982; XXIV, No. 1, "Two Actresses: Betty Chancellor and Claire Neufeld," pp. 180-197, 1983; XLIV, Nos. 1 & 2, "Aging Amelia," p. 347, 2003. Reprinted by permission from *The Massachusetts Review,* © 1982, 1983, 2003 The Massachusetts Review, Inc.

The frontispiece photograph of Doris Abramson directing student Jack Gianino in 1957 and front and back cover photographs are courtesy of Doris Abramson.

Library of Congress Cataloging-in-Publishing Data:
    Abramson, Doris E.
     Time will tell / Doris Abramson.
        p. cm.
     ISBN-13: 978-1-884540-81-3
     I. Title.
     PS3551.B718T56 2006
     811'.54--dc22

For Ann H. Kline
. . . and always
for Dorothy

Contents

A Few Poems and Some Prose

I have a few poems I've been writing for years. Two of them are the best poems I've never written. Each could become a short story—if I were capable of writing a short story. I once tried, and it was rejected for reasons I understood and still understand. Years later I discovered that one of the rejecting editors kept the story in his desk drawer to read now and then. I do, too.

Maybe someday I'll write short stories or sustain a prose memoir instead of folding memories into short poems. Time will tell.

If in the poems collected here I seem preoccupied with aging and with animals, it is not surprising. I am eighty years old, and I live in a house that is also home to three small dogs and five cats.

The prose selections are portraits of men and women I knew and admired and, yes, loved. They have all been, as the Irish say, gathered. Let them live again in these pages.

In his remarkable memoir *The View from 80* (1980), Malcolm Cowley wrote that at eighty "the last act has begun." He speaks of entering "the country of age." So here I am. I feel sure that Cowley would agree that we spend a lot of time looking back to earlier acts. These memories do, indeed, inform where we now stand.

Now I want to share jottings that show my interest in words. That's what verse and prose have in common, and I have been for a long time recording moments with words that seem to me worth sharing.

In the summer of 1990, I wrote down these words, spoken by a woman who was stepping out of a cool library, just as I was, into a hot day. "I mourn spring and fall, which we seem to miss entirely." So precise and so poetic. Not "miss" but "mourn"; after all, she was about to say "miss." It sounds like writing, not speaking, a sentence so carefully worded and said to a passing stranger.

"Let's not ask if we're going to church. Of course we're going to church. If it's Sunday, we're going to church." That's what Margo Rand said in 1988; she was then ninety-eight years old and was quoting her late husband, Frank Prentice Rand, saying that he said it shortly after they were married in 1923. The clock that a cousin gave them for a wedding present was still ticking sixty-five years later. There was always a moment when she would make a visitor stop to listen to the beautiful sound of the clock striking; it struck every fifteen minutes. Her stories always had a memorized quality, as if everything was on a tape. In old age, the tape often got stuck, and she said things two or three times and then got back on track. Until she was a hundred, she had the right responses, all arranged for the right occasion, the words and inflections just so. At the end of her time (she died at 104), the stories were all in a muddle, but she wasn't desperate; she didn't need to say it all any more. She seemed no longer anxious, no longer reciting for an audience. She was just getting ready for silence.

One afternoon—I think it was in Leominster—I jotted down notes based on a conversation between two elderly women who sat in a restaurant booth behind me. They had come from what they called an adult center—where they meet, though they may still have rooms and apartments and just go to the center for "recreation."

"I like the way you open your Sweet 'n' Low," one said almost flirtatiously. Then a discussion of Meals-on-Wheels and saving leftovers in the freezer. "You can have a meal for seventy-five cents. What the dickens!"

On the subject of salad bars: "The salads stay out and pick up something." Pause. "I don't know."

"When I go out at night, I see at night. Maybe I've got cat's eyes." Then a bit about the color of her eyes. "Blue? Green?"

"No," her friend answered. "Hazel. My grandfather had one blue eye and one brown. Elizabeth Taylor has purple eyes. I don't think there are many around."

One spoke of a "girl" who comes to the adult center, probably to lead them in exercises. "She wears a gym suit. A sweat suit?"

"That's not what they use for jogging, is it?"

"Some do."

One spoke of someone who was "putting on weight a mile a minute."

I'd have dialogue for a one-act play if I followed these two around for a few hours. Even a plot might emerge.

It's not, of course, only the old who provide stories. In the late sixties I was on an IRT subway in NYC one summer afternoon. All the seats were taken. There were only a few strap hangers or pole holders. We were a usual subway congeries—young, old, black, white, clean, dirty. Many were reading newspapers or paperbacks. Suddenly we could hear a high, sweet, tenor voice singing an old popular song, "So wrap your troubles in dreams, and dream your troubles away." We looked up to see a blind man with a cane, groping his way down the aisle.

He was in no way the kind of subway blind man of whom some say, "Bet he's a phony. Probably has more money than I have." He walked like a healthy young man. He wore no dark glasses to cover his eyes, for he had no eyes at all. His face was covered with scar tissue and completely devoid of eyes. He poked ahead with his stick, all the way singing hauntingly " . . . it's only gray for a day." What a long gray day for him!

What happened to all of us in the subway car was that we began to participate in a ritual act. One by one, as he passed, we each stood and put coins into his cap, which he didn't hold out but kept near his body, at the top of his cane. Some of us stumbled when we rose, several throats were cleared, and no one spoke.

When he reached the end of the car, a large workman put an arm around the shoulders of the young blind man and half carried him to the next car. "So wrap your troubles in dreams, and dream your troubles away." We went back to our newspapers and into ourselves.

And not too long ago I learned that the boy I danced with in high school—so gracefully that we were left alone on the dance floor for fellow students to applaud—that boy, old, but not really old, died. He had had to have his feet amputated, I was told. Diabetes. And when I heard the news, I wept, remembering the elegant way he'd dipped and swerved those years ago at the high school prom. He held me so carefully, making us move as dancers ideally should—flowing, easy, assured. Rest in peace, dear boy. You'll always dance in my dreams, and they'll always clear the floor to watch and wonder at our grace. They'll always applaud.

When Denis Johnston, the subject of one of my essays, came back to Mount Holyoke College (he'd been retired for many years) to receive an honorary degree in the spring of 1983, I went to see him in the room where he was staying. I found him poring over his own book (a bound manuscript at that time), *The Brazen Horn*. I had to interrupt his deep concentration on his own words. I'd prefer, I thought later, to be caught reading someone else's words, not my own. But that was in 1983. By now I know what a temptation it is to finger pages of one's own composition, to be reminded of accomplishments, to be reminded that one has existed. Remember Krapp listening to his tapes.

When I was teaching *Death of a Salesman* to an introduction-to-theater class, I had my students watch Dustin Hoffman as Willy Loman in a made-for-TV movie. After class, a student told me that Hoffman's Loman reminded him of his grandfather who had Alzheimer's disease. "He pats his hair, his face, the way Willy does, to make sure he's still here." Perhaps we write memoirs or personal poems to be sure we are still here.

They Should Be Thanked

Was there ever a monument made to them,
the gas-detecting canaries sent into mines
for the miners' sakes—for all our sakes
over time? A monument to canaries. How
do you make small monuments? By definition
monuments are massive. And for canaries?
The question of scale aside, these canaries
deserve recognition. Maybe someone will
write a song to be played on a solo flute.
They gave their little lives for us and
should be thanked. Or so I think.

Just When We Thought She Was Gone

Just when we thought she was gone
—we've heard coyotes in the night—
just when we started to name her past tense,
Isabel came home. No use to ask where she's
been. Just break out the cat food and say,
"Isabel's home! That's one cat we'll have
another day." Alive and here and hungry.

Lucy

Reaching claws to say she cares, she's
the only cat who wounds me. Drawing blood,
she purrs. I'm both angered (too strong a word?)
and pleased by her sudden attention. "Stop it,
Lucy. Just stop it right now." Until another day
when I pet the only cat, in a house full of cats,
who wounds me each time predictably.

Betsy's Paddy

Paddy. Does he miss her warmth that went away
the day she died with him beside her? That's what
death is, isn't it? Warmth goes, never to come again.
A cat can't curl beside the spirit and would leave soon,
I suspect, if not taken away from the woman it loved
in the warmth of life. Sensible cat will find another
place to be. But if Paddy dreams, he dreams of Betsy.
Of that I am sure.

Aging Amelia

Old dog, she still can feel her way
to the water bowl, still can ruminantly
chew with just a few remaining teeth, two
or three. She wobbles sometimes, and then
astonishes observers by skipping, by dancing,
keeping up with other dogs half her age. She's
a wonder, we say, and wonder what will lay her
low. I'll vote for skipping, for dancing.

Just In Case

Just now I saw Amelia lift a paw over a sill
that wasn't there. She did it neatly, carefully.
That's right. Better be cautious, old dog. The sill
could materialize at any time, and dogs don't have
canes to feel their way with at times like these.
To tell the truth, old folks with or without canes
could learn from you to step over any obstacle seeming
to present itself along the way. Just in case.
Old age has more than its share of surprises.

Good Night, Amelia

Looking around, bewildered at first,
she focuses—but where? on what?
She seems to sense direction but
whimpers at the thought that she
may be lost. "Oh, Amelia, we all are."
But that's no consolation to an old dog
trying to find her way—perhaps to bed,
perhaps to what we fear and she's spared
knowing. "Good night, Amelia. Good night."

For Elsie
or Art Is Where You Find It

Licking the screen. That little dog's
licking the screen! As if there's
sustenance there. Not fair, little dog,
this waste of deliberate action. Still
your licking is art of a kind. The strokes
show patterns of longing. That's art. Go on.
Lick the screen, little dog. I'll give you
biscuits to reward your patterns of longing.

Nearing Eighty

Nearing eighty, one expects to die
any day now. Look at the obits—
"dies at 80" appears time after time.
There are, of course, stories of
exceptions: "She's still quilting
at 90." "He's a father at 92." Or
someone's neighbor is the one she
asks for directions, for recipes and
advice. That one's 89. Oh, well—I
guess I'll accept 80 hopefully and
make of it what I can, given the
circumstances. Forget the obits. I'll
remember the lucky ones and what I have
to share, to pass on—if not recipes or
directions, at least a poem or two.

The Old Teacher's Plea

Would the pupils come back, please,
to tell who I am by telling me who I was
to them once. Please. If only a few would
bear witness to a moment in their lives when
I reached them in a way that has lasted. You see,
I doubt my memory. Please, pupils, come back to me.
And make it soon. Time erases time itself in time.

Remembering

The old woman strokes her withering legs,
remembering them shapely and admired,
remembering too when she was told her feet
were pretty. They were. Not gnarled like now.
How long has it been since others praised
her legs, her feet—herself if truth be told?
"Those were the days," she sighs—and rising
almost dances.

Just a Suggestion

There's a moment in many a day when I say,
"If this is it, so be it. What I see now—a view
of maples, a comforting snow, sunsets (oh yes sunsets),
what I hear—often Mozart, though silence at times—is
fine by me. When I'm gathered, let it be at a time like
these. Please." It's not mine, of course, to say when.
Just a suggestion before the Amen.

Who Cuts In?

Who cuts in, into the dance—in time?
Death, that's who (sorry, that's Who).
Where will I be? Twirling? I think not.
Stumbling to a rhythm I haven't heard yet
is more likely. I hope to die in action,
moving, if slightly, on to the next dance
(make that next Dance). Not yet please;
I'm still trying out new steps.

Obits

Have you thought whose obituary yours will nestle by?
He leaves a wife, she leaves a husband of how many years?
Longtime companions appear where not considered appropriate
earlier. And look, a baby scarcely here but acknowledged.
Teenagers dead in a one-car crash, after the prom. Cancer
claims someone at twenty who's accomplished more than others
longer lived. And you? Born, did some things, won some
prizes. You'll leave the scene in your way and be recorded
among strangers who met their end in their fashion. You're
related in death who'd never even met when alive.

Lucky Stiff

After the many indignities of dying –
for him it took a long, long time –
came the peace and quiet of death.
At the wake, an old crony from
the Soldiers Home, pausing at the
casket's rim, was heard to mutter
two words in parting: "Lucky stiff."

Funeral services were held on a
cold memorial hill. Only a few in
attendance, mostly fellow Legionnaires.
Prayers were mumbled, tributes paid.
A boy from Catholic High played taps
as if for the first time. "Lucky stiff"
could well have been an appropriate Amen.

The Dead

Do they hang around in
    heaven's hallways,
waiting to be dreamed?

Loss

for Anne Halley (1928-2004)

I read the paper today. She didn't.
I saw the sun set. She couldn't.
What about that? What about loss?
Anne I thought would be here for
all the days I'll know. But now
I've read the paper when she didn't,
and I've seen a sunset she couldn't see.

On Hearing of the Death
of Donald Justice (1926-2004)

"Did Justice die?," I asked
(knowing lower-case had died
earlier and often). To learn
the poet had died stopped
my heart a moment. He was young
when I was young. I've listened with
attentive pleasure to his words.
Bless you, Justice. We never met, but
bless your poet's heart all the same.

Joan

for Joan Heller (1925-2004)

"Joan, where are you?," I asked.
Unable to answer, she sent word
along a breeze from lilacs, saying
"With you and with others who love me."
That's where she is and that's where
we know she'll stay. "Farewell, Joan.
And welcome home. Yes. Welcome home."

That Perfect Time of Day

This is that perfect time of day—
not evening yet but not afternoon.
French would give us crepuscular, but
that isn't right somehow. Quiet descends
at our house. How about yours? Sun lingers
but doesn't deign to stay. Too late. Sorry.
A light settles like no other on a day that
outlasts itself for just a while. And we—
we're beneficiaries of a moment extended almost
to evening but not quite. Afternoon to evening:
day on its way to night.

I Saw Her Wince

for Adrienne Rich

I saw her wince when I said, "I rarely finish
poems I'm reading in magazines these days."
And she was right. I shouldn't judge a poem
partially any more than I'd criticize a play
if I left at intermission. Oh, dear—I
do that, too; though more reluctantly, having
paid a price for tickets far beyond the cost of
magazines. My leaving either—the printed page,
the lighted stage—is, of course, a critical act.
And I cheat myself, not poet, playwright, or
performer, in missing perhaps a phrase or
maybe a gesture I'd remember all my days.

Remembering the Common Reader Bookshop

I miss the Thompsons on Sunday afternoons, and I
miss the Murphys coming by—father, mother, daughters.
I miss the music student commuting somewhere, looking
for scores she could afford. We had them and sold them
cheap. I looked for her late Friday afternoons.

I miss bending and stretching to shelve books by
alphabet—old favorites skimmed with pleasure and
oddities discovered, perhaps to be read in time.

I miss the bookshop, a place to meet old and make new
friends—some human, some bound. I miss them all
as I recall bright and rainy afternoons.

Our Trees Are Tapped

Spring, 2003

There's hope. Our trees are tapped.
With so much snow, we wondered if
the ritual would abide. It did.
Our trees are tapped. Tappers waded
through knee-deep drifts to make it
happen. Our trees are tapped. Sap
will rise to waiting buckets, in an
annunciation of spring. Our trees are tapped.

Spring 2005

It's sad to think that we won't see
our trees tapped this year. We'll miss
the sight of buckets hung in hopeful array
on trees in our front yard. Humans had
human reasons for forsaking old maples that
'til now had been the source of special
pleasures in the spring. Oh, yes, spring will
arrive as always—but without the announcement
we'd come to expect: metal buckets with
small sounds made no other way.

This Day

I waited for the leaf to land, an early fall leaf
making its graceful way from tree to bush below.
And then the surprise: having landed, it took
no time at all to ascend beautifully—a butterfly,
a butterfly disguised as a leaf. No matter to me.
Beauty arrives when and where it arrives. This day
it was a butterfly.

Love Poem I

I don't like it when she's not here.
Can't fill the silence her absence brings
with music, with phone calls, with attention to
dogs or cats. She's not here, and I don't like
being alone. Wonder how she feels when I'm away.

Love Poem II

All the turns we might have taken,
all the vows we might have made,
hardly ever come to mind.
As luck would have it, where we are
is where we're pleased to be.

Love Poem III

I hope I don't die in the back room
when she's in the kitchen. I pray
we're together that day. It's hard, though,
to set the scene of one's dying. Maybe
Frost was right: "something has to be left
to God."

Continuing to Clip

for Kate, Connie, et al

At what point do I stop clipping papers for
"quotes" I'll use in classes I no longer teach?
Never, I suspect. "Oh, they'll want to know,"
I surmise, forgetting they're not here any more.
So what? Who's to say when they'll reappear as
students of my students, now teachers, who may be
teaching what I taught—or some version anyway.
Reason enough to go on clipping.

Prayer

a lyric for Carolyn Brown Senier

O Lord, come when dew is on the ground
or come when trees are bending low with snow.
Come to free our hearts from aching. Come here.
If ever you come, come now.

Faith

When any Faith gets loud,
it loses me.
I like the mumbled prayers
of old believers.
I like a timid crossing
at the breast.
When panoply becomes the way
a Faith is seen,
it loses me.

The Babies

Our friends have children bringing children
into the world. I fear the future for us and
surely for them. Can't cry "Stop!" That's to say
nay to everything, to give up. (Oh, it's a temptation.)
But this spinster says, "Maybe we'll last."
All we can do is pray for the babies.

9 / 11

I went to a neighborhood bar to watch
the tragedy on TV. Picture was clear,
sound OK. An audience of garrulous old men
prompted by current events to reminisce—and
young men watching the news intently, quietly
smoking, and drinking their beers. Setting a
tray of glasses on the bar, a bus boy named Seth
asked of the air, "What can we do?" Who could say?
The old men made a stab at answering—something about
"Show them." Something about "Jesus." His name's
evoked at times like these. In fact, we all said
"Jesus" at one moment, as if on one breath, whatever
was on our individual minds.

La Ronde / Manhattan Merry-Go-Round

Once, going to meet her current lover at the Guggenheim,
she caught the eye of a woman who returned her glance,
a woman who for a whole afternoon was her pleasure,
her joy. A woman with no attachments and wanting none.
She never went back to the man who had seemed
the perfect way to fill spaces in her busy days.
Oh, she always went back to her husband. He was
habit, he was fun, the one she'd bargained for.
He'd have said she was the one he'd won in spite of
outward show.

At academic conventions, colleagues buying her drinks
are diversions merely, the same as conquests he makes
at his meetings, buying and selling, then flaunting
what they laugh at at home. They are a cozy pair,
sharing stories gained by going abroad for a while.

We could feel sorry for the used ones, I suppose,
but all in all the arrangement's admirable
for pleasures brought to many—from time to time.

In a Dream

She was young and wearing red.
I turned to someone then and said,
"Doesn't she look like Miriam Hopkins?"

That was my dream, and dreams begin somewhere.
For the quote if not the coat, this one began
in high school, began with Beth at a desk in
the afternoon sun, posing (it turns out) forever.

Leah

Her last name escapes me. I knew her
when she was a child, when we were both
children. How will I find her again?
Not in the phone book, not on the Net.
Leah. Lovely Leah who came into my life
dancing—at the age of twelve or maybe
thirteen. In a class where partners were
chosen for us, I was lucky to have Leah
at arms' length and there for my counting,
counting steps I remember 'til now. "One-two-three,
two-two-three." Leah Who? It's enough, I guess,
to hold a memory if not a whole name at arms' length:
a dancing girl named Leah.

Poor Pretty Nancy

She fell in a "fit"—someone called it—
on the study-room floor. Pretty, popular
Nancy, cheerleader and best dancer in our
class, lying writhing on our study-room floor.
I'd like to say I rushed to help. Someone did
(someone always does). But I ran home to ask
my mother, "If I take a fit, can we move? Can we
move to Kentucky?" Why Kentucky? Farthest away from
New England, I suppose, in my mind at the moment.
(Wonder what we were reading in English class.)
Mother agreed, knowing she was pretty safe in doing
so. My need was to avoid what? Embarrassment, I guess.
Not to be like poor, pretty Nancy, lying writhing
on our study-room floor.

The Old Bachelor

Do you remember the old bachelor—
old as we saw him with childhood's eyes—
who inspected his neat handkerchief after
blowing his nose into it nicely? And how
he replaced it then, folded, into his jacket
pocket? His mother, I imagine, washed each
snot-smeared square and ironed it flat for
folding into its proper place. Her son
counted on its being there all her days.

Wonder what happened to the old bachelor
after his mother's demise. I'd like to think
he discovered Kleenex, but rituals die hard.
He may have married and to this day examines
handkerchiefs laundered and ironed by his wife.

That Quiet Man

I hope he yelled, that quiet man who had
surgery when he broke both legs "on the job."
Reticent Yankee, he never complained of heights
or long hours suspended in often unfriendly winds.
He seemed at ease, at home up there against the sky.
He did what he was hired to do: trimmed branches,
lifted heavy wires into place, often off-balance
of necessity. And then the accident, the ambulance,
the operation. They say we find words under anesthesia
we were never known to know. Wonder what obscenities
that quiet man found. Mostly I hope he yelled.

A Cure for a Cold

A Mafia beau of my friend Pat,
singer extraordinaire, taught me
just one thing: "Put butter in
your coffee—black coffee—whenever
you have a cold." About that,
I'll admit he was right.

The Tattoo

She honored her grandmother with a tattoo—
just her dates. 1930-2002, on her upper arm.
"Couldn't go to the funeral," she explained.
"Too far away." But this would say forever
her love. You can't peel it off, can't pluck
it off; it's there for all time. The best
justification for a tattoo I've ever heard,
a clear and indelible statement of love.

But, Maya

"Maya. But, Maya," Elie Wiesel said in
public conversation with Maya Angelou—
before an audience of two thousand. He
bleated the words, trying to interrupt the
articulate flow of her opinions. "Maya. But,
Maya . . . " Today I remember little of what
they said, only his attempts to be heard.

Marilyn Monroe

In memory she's lived longer than
she did in reality. (Reality? Whose?)
"Pre-eminent sex symbol" critics called her,
naming her next in line after Mae West.
Truth to tell, sad Marilyn's won over
tough Mae, whose sexiness had too much humor
to last in the way we speak today of sex. Laughs
don't make it over the long run. It takes
the poignant to truly impress. Tears from laughter
can be brushed away. Tears from a life like Marilyn's
smudge makeup, cause coughs. All unsightly. And now
critics speak of her "posthumous career," meaning
all the years we've worshipped a sad face, a lost
look in eyes not focused on where she is but where
she'll be: alone and lost forever at last—
worshipped but alone.

A Letter from Miami

"How nice the trash men are," she wrote.
"How attentive." After complaints about
stocks and bonds and vintage wines, she added—
his aged mother added—to her usual litany of
complaints: "How nice the trash men are.
How attentive." She'd never have said those words
in New York. Must be the climate—or maybe her age.

The City

Isn't it lovely? Isn't it nice?
Here in the city I never think twice
before walking ways not walked before.
To happen on by-ways is never a bore.
Any street new to me's a treat I admit
(that is, of course, if it's lit).
Isn't it lovely? Isn't it nice?
The city's variety is what I call spice.

Two Actresses: Betty Chancellor and Claire Neufeld

In the early sixties, Betty Johnston and Claire Volbach may
have met at Louis' Supermarket in Amherst, Massachusetts.
They may even have smiled at each other (I like to think so)
in recognition of something heightened or extended about
their performances as housewives shopping routinely, each
in her fashion. Even then I knew that fashion to be calculated,
to be exempt from the humdrum, the expected. They reached
for pork chops and tested melons with hands accustomed to
theatrical gestures. I did not know then, but I believe now that
these two women, these accomplished actresses, brought a
special awareness to their social roles, one of which was "faculty wife." They were what Erving Goffman called cynics.

> It should be understood that the cynic, with all
> his professional disinvolvement, may obtain unpro-
> fessional pleasures from his masquerade, experi-
> encing a kind of gleeful spiritual aggression from
> the fact that he can toy at will with something his
> audience must take seriously.[1]

In a period when we assumed we could "type" a faculty
wife, wearer of white gloves and pourer of tea, we tended
to say of Betty or Claire, "Well, she's not your typical faculty
wife." Mary McCarthy and Alison Lurie should have convinced us that these exceptions tested rules that were rarely
observed in toto and clearly broken by lively spirits from the
beginning. (Remember Mabel Loomis Todd.) Perhaps the
theater wives were more gleeful in their spiritual aggression
because more aware of their audience. I was a member of that
audience, but only recently have I thought about the lives of
these two women before I met them, when they were per-
forming on stage.

And now that fantasy has opened the door of recollection, I can see their husbands waiting for them. Betty's Denis (Denis Johnston) used to speak of "taxiing" her to Louis'. Sometimes he walked behind her, tall and useless, respecting her decision-making, studying the scene rather than the produce. More often he waited in the car or went away on other errands, returning at an agreed-upon time. Claire's Walther (Walther Volbach), looking every inch the Herr Doktor Professor that he was, chose to sit at the front of the store. (Where did he find a chair? Perhaps there was a ledge.) There he waited, reading the *Times*, opening and folding it elaborately with his long fingers, until Claire had finished her meticulous shopping. In fantasy I see the two men greet with a nod, sensing an affinity of husbandry, perhaps not even knowing that they shared more. In the early sixties, Denis Johnston, Irish playwright, was chairman of the Smith College Theater Department. Walther Volbach, formerly a stage director in Germany and now a United States citizen, taught theater history at the University of Massachusetts. Both impressive men, but I will leave them at Louis', caught in the amber of my fancy, for they are not my subject. They serve only this purpose here: they have interesting wives. The men must wait in the car or read the *Times*; the focus is on the women.

Before they came to America, Claire in 1938 and Betty ten years later, they had been professional actresses. Claire Neufeld was born in 1985 in Vienna and had a short career (about six seasons) in German and Austrian theaters. Betty Chancellor, born in 1910 in Dublin, had a longer career (twenty years), principally in Ireland and England. The parallel interviews that follow are the result of my talking to Betty in Ireland in the spring of 1982 and to Claire in Amherst the following summer.

Betty Chancellor

Waiting for me to ask my first question, Betty seemed to withdraw, to disappear into her cigarette smoke. She seemed to be preparing herself inwardly, privately. She is still an actress, I thought, and an interview is an opening of a sort. Describing her reactions to first nights over forty years ago, Micheal MacLiammóir wrote: "In Betty a curious vanishing process takes place, the childish features grow smaller, meeker and more supplicating, they recede into distant unknown places."[2]

What are you thinking about, Betty?

That I am only half a person when I'm not acting. I am a dull person. I love taking on the colors of others. I always know what people are like. Micheal said once that my only spark of genius was a sense of character. I don't think I would ever have been a star, as I wasn't enough interested in putting across my personality.

MacLiammóir said that you were "born for the stage." Where did it all begin, your interest in the theater?"

I grew up in an atmosphere of theater. Daddy loved the theater. He and his sisters and brothers did a play, *The Belle of Dalkey Island.* Daddy played a pirate. Aunt Lily was the heroine. They did the play on Dalkey Island and had a special train laid on to bring out their guests from Dublin.

Tell me more about them.

The Chancellors lived first in Sandycove, then in Dalkey, near the railway. They had a lovely house in Sandycove going right down to the sea, but the drainage was so bad that some of the children (including my father) got typhoid, and one of them died. So grandfather built a grand house near the railway. It was a lovely house. Only this year it was demolished to make room for lots of flats. It was always let when I knew it, to my sorrow, and eventually the bank got it.

Tell me about your mother.

My mother was a singer, trained at the Royal College of Music. Her father was left a fortune because he was the first Protestant child of a mixed marriage. His father was a K.C. and member of Parliament for Durham County, who married a Stack of Limerick. The Stacks divided up—some turned Prod including the ones I got to know during World War II.

My great grandmother was a Catholic, and the one with all the cash was a rich spinster. Instead of teaching Grandfather something about money, sent him into the army. He never fired a shot in his life. He resigned out of boredom and lost all his money, mostly through bad advice. He reached the rank of Lieutenant Colonel, and Mummy and her sisters— her brothers were both in the army—had to earn. One of my aunts wrote romance novels and made quite a bit of money.

And your earliest experience in the theater?

My mother sang in an amateur singing society, and I went on as a page in Gilbert and Sullivan. I remember carrying ladies' trains in *Gondoliers* and a sword in *The Mikado*—for Henry Lytton. I would have been between ten and thirteen or fourteen. At the age of twelve or so I went in the Gaiety to pick up a child's part. Fourteen was the legal age. Father found out, but he didn't mind, as the parts were few and far between. Gwennie in *The Man from Blankley's* I vaguely remember.

In 1938, just before I went to Micheal and Hilton (The Dublin Gate Theater), I was in the Drama League's production of *Cradle Song*. Mrs. Yeats paid me. I couldn't believe it—two guineas! I bought evening shoes.

I want to break in to read a description of you by Micheal MacLiammóir. He is writing at what he calls "the edge of a decade," 1929-30, when you were all of nineteen years old.[3]

Our most exciting discovery that year was Betty

Chancellor. She was a curious little creature with smoky brown hair that grew with heedless subtlety round a pale childish face with shapely supplicating eyes, a small good-tempered mouth which was kept appropriately dewy and crimson but never too much so, and a brief and unexpected little nose that gave her a sisterly feeling towards Amy in *Little Women.* Her pathos was facile, but real and irresistible, and her comedy gift a delight, as pure and brilliant as crystal. She spoke with a purring Dublin drawl that misled many Irish and all English people into thinking she lived in a pleasant coma; she wore an air of helplessness that secured for her an indefinite number of slaves, and had a way of pushing her hair behind her ear when she was addressed and murmuring, 'What, please?' in a veiled and blissful perplexity, and you wondered for a while why she did this so often. Then you found out that she was rather deaf, and this seemed to explain a lot about Betty, for she was as soft and muffled and remote and confiding as a kitten, and although she could be as wicked as green satin you knew she must feel apart sometimes.

But her deafness never affected her work, except to make her concentrate more seriously than any of us, for she was born for the stage.[4]

I have to ask about your deafness and its effect on your career.

When it became apparent in my teens that I was deaf, my mother insisted that I be trained as a secretary. "No one wants a deaf actress." "No one wants a deaf secretary either," I replied.

I went to the Cambridge Festival Theater, I think it was

in 1933. They didn't mind that I suffered from deafness. The deafness was osteosclerosis, shared also by Queen Alexandra and Margaret Sullavan.

A nurse who was giving me treatment in London gave Ronald Jeans my name. He spotted my comic sense. The play was *Ghost for Sale*; it was a flop, but A. E. Mathews and Robert Edison were in it, and I got great notices. He had written me a lovely part after only one meeting! The stage manager pulled me aside and told me, "Good parts need good playin'." I took it for a compliment.

I used to learn everyone's part. On the West End they were very helpful. If there was a silent cue, they flashed a light.

Radio was a blessing. I did a MacNeice play, *The Heartless Giant*, with Peter Ustinov and Dylan Thomas. Music by Benjamin Britten. I was in a radio version of *Cinderella* by MacNeice—played an ugly sister.

Did you always play in comedies?

No. But I was a comedian first and foremost.

How about Shakespeare? I know you've played Ophelia.

I hadn't the voice for Shakespeare. I was not a good Ophelia, but I had success with the role in Cairo in '37.

Yeats stood up for me at the Peacock Theater, during our first run of *Hamlet* with me as Ophelia. (Meriel Moore[5] had gone to South Africa.) He got up at a press conference and called me "this wonderful little girl."

When I played Stella in *Yahoo*, a play about Swift, Yeats saw me on the bus and said to me, "I did not recognize you—so small, so young." Here she imitates his intoning the words slowly, deliberately.

In the Thirties, Paul Robeson was acting in London. Did you ever work with him?

He was more in the twenties. In 1937 I rehearsed *Sanders of the River* at Drury Lane. Robeson did the film but I think not the play. Not then anyway. I only rehearsed it, as H. M. Tennant took me out of it to play in *Spring Meeting*. That was by Molly Keane and John Perry. It ran a year, but I had to leave, on account of a baby, Jeremy, on the way, after six months.

Do you think of the roles you might have played, the ones you missed?

Oh, yes. I missed Queen Victoria in *Victoria Regina* by Laurence Houseman. I had temporarily left the Gate when they did it. That's a role I could have done. And any part in *The Women*. Even the gym instructress. I will always remember that gym lady giving the nasty woman harder and harder exercises. Finally the bitch says, "Do you think I'm a horse?" "You're getting warm, Mrs. Fowler!" *Curtain.* They were going to do it for Longford Productions. All agreed it was well written. But no roles for the men in the company. Too bad.

I'm glad to hear you mention an American play, though I would expect to hear about Lillian Hellman before Clare Boothe Luce.

I played in Hellman's *Watch on the Rhine* when I was about six months pregnant of Rory. He was born in March, 1946, and when he was about two months old we moved back to England. I also missed the part of the maid in the Thornton Wilder play *The Skin of Our Teeth*. Sabrina. I was getting too fat for a bathing dress! The part was played by Vivien Leigh in London and by Tallulah in New York.

Any other roles you dream about playing?

I didn't get Nina in *The Sea Gull* in 1931, because the leading lady insisted on playing when Meriel got Juliet. I played it later in Cambridge.[5]

I would have liked to play Hedwig in *The Wild Duck*.

Speaking of Ibsen, do you have a favorite Shaw role?

I loved both Cleopatra and Elly Dunn in *Heartbreak House*.

They were so easy to play.

What was the story about your being carried on as the Newly Born in Shaw's Back to Methuselah?

I was supposed to be carried on in the egg on a trestle, but the supers carrying the trestle were weak and trembling and nearly dropped me in the egg down a flight of stairs. So I hopped into the egg from behind the altar.

I met you in 1950. By then you and Denis and the boys were in residence in South Hadley. Your role was "faculty wife." How did that feel?

It was traumatic to go from actress to faculty wife. Somebody's got to give, and I made the decision to give. After all, Denis and Shelah[6] had stronger egos than I have. I wanted my children with me. I gave up the stage in 1948.

As for faculty wife, I had to improvise. I had to be careful. There were intellectual snobs among the wives. A lot of them were teaching. I resented them being so patronizing to someone without a degree. In Europe one just "went on the stage."

If they weren't teaching, they were so domesticated! Mary Ann Sprague, though very domesticated, had a brain. She was very kind and taught me a lot of domestic tips. She was also grand to my children. She should have written really. She had a summa from Smith. She gave herself over to her family. I give her full marks, bless her.

Kitty Canfield taught me about parties, how to give them. The Morgans were good friends, too, especially Katie.

What was the story you used to tell about Edward Albee in South Hadley?

Denis and I were at a party given for Albee who had agreed sometime before to lecture at Mount Holyoke and who kept his promise even though the date was, I believe, opening night of *Who's Afraid of Virginia Woolf?* in New York. It was a respectable party given by Miss Ludington.[7] There was a dark rascally Irishman on the faculty. He had a silly wife named Jane—bobbing red curls. Two dreads for children. As usual in America, I went into the kitchen. There was Jane in hysterics at the sink. She hated her husband and was crying into the sink. Denis and I were calming her down. Albee was in the other room. It was a scene from his play exactly.

You and I saw that play together. We sat in a box. That's when you first told me this story.

I don't remember ever being able to tell Albee, but it was an extraordinary scene. Especially for a Ludington party.

I know that the little acting you found time to do in the United States was with college students, at Amherst College. How did it feel to be a professional among amateurs?

I was frightened out of my wits. It was like acting with drunks. They simply weren't serious.

I should never have done *Candida*. Intolerable! And I didn't like the role of the mother in *You Never Can Tell*. It fizzles out.

When one of the actresses had a car accident, I went on as Mrs. Vanderbilt in Denis's *The Golden Cuckoo*—without knowledge of the third act. No rehearsal because the boys had a football match. Because of that match I had never seen the Court or Post Office scene! It was a nightmare. I believe the director, Ed Pettet, was unhelpful because he wanted to play my part.

You are one of the best storytellers I know, Betty. Is it a substitute for acting?

A doctor said to me once, when I missed acting, "Make up things when you're doing the housework." I've done it. I have recited endless poetry and plays to the detriment of my cooking. The storytelling is instinctive. I just don't know where that comes from.

Some would say it comes from being Irish, but that's too easy.

These days I know you are homesick for America, but I remember reading about your being homesick for Dublin when you were in London. You told MacLiammóir: "I'm homesick. Ya know what it is, it's the voices. Oh, God, the voices!"[8]

Alas, I no longer have much feeling for Dublin. Today it is being destroyed by people on the make, and drugs and crooks about, in spite of the ostentatious religious feeling.

That sounds like American cities, too.

I suppose. When I remember America, I remember the friendliness of people. I remember apple orchards. I loved it.

And yet it was in America that you rarely acted.

I know. And I am only half a person when I am not acting.

Claire Neufeld

In the Volbachs' comfortable living room, in a modern condominium in Amherst, there is a portrait of Claire Neufeld as a serious, pretty seventeen-year-old. She looks in control but not comfortable. When I asked who painted it and when, Claire said the artist was Rudolf Fuchs, a well-known Viennese portrait painter. "He painted the House of Hapsburg children," she added. "He happened to be a friend of my older brother and asked me to model. In 1912." When I said how much I liked the portrait, her reply was very definite: "I don't. I never liked it. It didn't predict my looks, though the painter told me I'd 'grow into it.' I looked always different from that painting. And then I didn't like seeing myself hanging on a wall."

It is obvious to me that she still does not like it. The painting dominates one wall, but she turns her back to it rather emphatically. Her walk is less certain than it was even a few years ago, but her gestures are strong.[9] Her favorite way to punctuate a conversation is to raise her arms high before her, confirming points she makes with precise movements of her expressive hands.

When I met you in the early sixties, you had already been in America for twenty years, living most of that time in Texas. You had then and you have now a lovely accent. I especially like that liquid "r." I wish I could have heard you speaking German from the stage. I'll have to settle for hearing about those days. How long were you active in the theater?

For approximately six years. And I got amazingly good notices. I kept clippings until I moved from Texas to New England. Then I threw them out.

Threw them all out?

Yes. It seemed vain to save them. Anyway, they were in German. But I kept them very long—'til they were yellow.

Tell me about your family.

I was born in Vienna in 1895. My father was a businessman who traveled a lot. Both sides of my family were non-practicing, assimilated Jews. My mother was from a well-to-do family, manufacturers. They owned a leather factory. She was one of twelve children. Her brothers were educated for the professions. My mother was the oldest of three girls in the family and was married off at the age of nineteen to provide an opportunity of a suitor for the younger ones.

My mother greatly resented the fact that girls were not supposed to sit down and read; so she sometimes locked herself in the bathroom with one of her brother's books (he was a medical student). I am sure that her own experiences made her determined to have all her children well educated. With seven of them—four boys, then an interval of seven years followed by my three-years-older sister, me, and my brother—this was not an easy task. As it happens sometimes in large families, there were two sets of children. The three younger ones were close.

All of us learned to play the piano, and my little brother played the violin. To be Viennese is to be musical.

How about your interest in the theater?

I went to a private school. There I loved to recite. Once, I remember, my girlfriend and I chose a dialogue between two women, from Goethe's *Torquato Tasso*, earning great applause for our recitation.

From time to time the Burgtheater offered the upper-class students tickets on the balcony for a nominal price. Whenever I could, I grabbed one. Also my family had a season ticket for the opera. Our subscription entitled us to pre-purchase two assigned seats on the fourth balcony (the cheapest in the house) every other day. We had the odd-numbered ones of the month.

We went to the theater, the opera, or concerts, all the time. It was a Viennese habit. Vienna was a city of theater and music.

But something led you to a career in the theater.

When the war broke out in the fall of 1914, the easy-going life in Vienna gradually changed—especially for us teenagers. We girls had been trained to become housewives. We suddenly realized that we had better prepare to make a living, to become independent though brought up to be at home.

My sister had no trouble. She was musical, very gifted at the piano, and soon became a successful piano teacher. She also took up voice lessons—the Italian method—and proved to be very gifted once again. I was brooding, not knowing what to do with myself, worrying about my future, about the war. "Claire has to take voice lessons," said one of the older brothers. But I couldn't keep a tune. Fortunately, the voice teacher had a sister who was an actress. She suggested that some of us, who seemed to her talented, take dramatic lessons.

How did you feel? Do you remember?

Outside of my family and a small circle of friends I was always rather shy, unaware of being quite attractive. I was very emotional but couldn't get it out, couldn't express it. Suddenly, with dramatic lessons, all my emotions came out—through words from Goethe and Schiller. I was determined to go on to further training. All of a sudden I could give. I was not so quiet anymore.

You came out of your shell, your reticence.

Yes. And I had then some success with boys. I was, I suppose, attractive, but I never liked my looks. One young man wrote poems and sent them to me when he was in the army. Through him I met people—one of them a friend of Kafka.

Another young man I met during the war, when I was still taking private lessons, told me I must go to the Reinhardt School in Berlin. He told me I must get out of my bourgeois family. I was still timid, not convinced I could do it. But I did arrange for a first audition. It's a feature of mine that, though shy, in an emergency I can do it.

So you took the young man's advice.

Toward the end of the war I visited a cousin in Berlin and went to the Reinhardt School where I was auditioned by seven directors/teachers to see if I would be accepted by the school. I made it clear that I should be considered for the second year. I knew my mother couldn't afford more than one year of the two-year course. I was forced to be strong.

Do you remember what you used for an audition piece?

Something from Schiller's *Maria Stuart*, I think. I always liked the tragic roles, romantic tragedy. At that time I would have been suited for the jugendlich sentimentale roles. That after the ingénue and before heroine parts.

What about character parts?

That's a separate field. But we're getting ahead of the story. I had first to go to school before being hired by a theater company.

I was accepted at the secondary level and started classes in September, 1918. The war was over in November of that year, but I was in Berlin during the whole Revolution. I was, by the way, called the Red Claire.

Oh? Did you have red hair? Or were you "red" politically?

No to the red hair. Politically—no, too. I just fought for my own rights. I was red in the sense of fiery. The Deutsche

Theater, where we studied acting, was in the middle of shooting. My room was at the other end of Berlin, and I came in by train. One day the school intended to close down, and I objected. I insisted on getting my lessons in spite of the shooting. I had paid!

That's what I call determination.

I needed this year of acting training. I was not entirely satisfied with the teaching. I wanted more speech training and sought out private speech lessons. I was completely absorbed. Of course, I should add, we had complimentary tickets to some performances and all dress rehearsals in the three Reinhardt theaters. I admired everything I saw. It was a good part of my study.

Once when I was still in school I was chosen to replace an ailing actress in a performance of *Dies Irae* by the Austrian dramatist Anton Wildgans. It was on short notice, without rehearsal. The part was a deaf-mute youngster with some actions around her partner, Conrad Veidt.

There's a name I know. He ended up in Hollywood playing handsome villains, usually Nazis.

We two were the only ones on stage, he lying on a couch. I probably went in front of him. He whispered: "Get out of my way. The audience wants to see me, not you."

Well, that's an education of a sort.

I remember another time when the director of the school called me in to meet Max Reinhardt's leading dramaturg. When I entered the room, the director asked the visitor, "Is she pretty enough for you?" I fled. I found out later they were looking for someone to play—opposite?—in contrast to Leopoldine Konstantine, a famous leading lady, in the play *The Star* by Hermann Bahr. They wanted a Viennese girl. It would have been a good part for me.

Who got the part?

Mady Christians, a tall American girl.

She was in Hollywood, too.

My director bawled me out afterwards, saying Mady was awful in it. Here was an example of my being a coward in spite of the fact that I was a fighter. Actually, I was furious that these men did not consider my talent, just my looks.

And at the end of the year?

There were several openings for beginners at theaters in a number of German cities. I was called in to the Stuttgart Theater, where I was engaged at the state theater for one year (1919-1920).

I played some nice little parts. My first bigger one was in Tolstoy's *Living Corpse.* I was, I believe, very good. We had no real rehearsals. Just go on, come off. I played a gypsy girl in a nightclub. I had to play the lute and sing. I was so excited, so immersed in the role that I took the lute off with a huge gesture, hitting some glasses off the table and spilling their contents on the trousers of the leading man who cursed me. I was scared to death. But the director liked it! When he came from the audience after that act, he said, "Neufeld, you did a wonderful job."

Later on, in the same play, I was supposed to resist being taken off stage by my gypsy parents, and I pushed back more realistically than required. They had to take all their strength to get me off. Again a rebuke.

I needed more years to get over the excitement. I needed to get it into my head.

You hadn't reached the point of knowing why you were doing what you were doing. But you were succeeding, weren't you?

I was beginning in Stuttgart to get proud of myself. There were three beginners, and of them I was the only one chosen for a second year. Then an offer came from Meiningen. I was offered leading roles, in my second year.

In Meiningen (1920-1921) I received word that a Berlin director wanted to see me perform. I was to let him know when I had a role for him to see. I wrote him when I was scheduled to play Gretchen in *Faust*. The production was to have an entirely new mise-en-scène, hence a lot of rehearsals. The part was given to me and then taken away when an older actress asked the general manager who was to direct it to let her play Gretchen—because she expected to get flowers on stage. He begged me to let her have it, promising me the role of Louisa in Schiller's *Kabale und Liebe*. As usual, I gave in. I had to write to Berlin. The answer came back: "You come to Berlin and audition for us."

Did you go?

Yes. I was engaged at the Berlin Schiller Theater (1921-1922) for my field, my stage category, the judendlich sentimentale. I was entitled to play several leading roles a season in that category. Thus I played the Princess Eboli in *Don Carlos*, Natalie in Kleist's *Prinz von Hamburg*, the daughter (I forget her name) in Calderon's *Alcal de Zalamea*. And some parts in modern plays.

The Schiller Theater was not one of the really good theaters and at the end of 1922 it went bankrupt. The Berlin State Theater took it over, and we lost our jobs.

What happened to Claire Neufeld?

When the ensemble was dismissed, I went back to Vienna, got an agent, and started over.

The season of 1923-1924 I was acting at the Municipal Theater of Bamberg, and there I met Walther Volbach. I was cast as Titania in *A Midsummer Night's Dream*, and Walther was to play Oberon. He was an opera director, only substituting for an ailing actor. Then he himself fell ill at dress rehearsal!

Very romantic. How long did you stay in Bamberg?

I played there that season and married Walther on December 27, 1924. I was ready to marry and have never regretted it.

That's quite a statement from an actress whose early career was so promising. Are there roles you wish you had had a chance to play?

Yes, Juliet. I wanted to play Juliet. I got an offer when I was already married. It came from one of the smaller state theaters. There are many in Germany. They wanted to look me over—a kind of audition. I talked it over with Walther. He thought it unethical to take the part. They might have wanted to keep me.

What was your next move?

In the fall of 1925 we went to Switzerland, where Walther was engaged as the leading stage director at the Zürich Opera House. This ended my life as an actress and began my life as a director's wife—full of exciting moments, disappointment, worries, and triumph.

From Zürich we moved to Danzig, then a free city between Poland and Germany, a sore spot on the political map. The dominant population was German, but one had to travel through Poland to get to it. One felt as though living in exile.

After two years we decided to return to Germany. Berlin of course was the place to make contacts. There was the problem, though, how to show your work. There is no audition possible for a director. Sheer luck would have it that the Kroll Opera, one of the state opera houses in Berlin, offered Walther the opportunity to direct the premiere of Gluck's *Iphigenia auf Tauris*. The production was more or less considered an experiment: a lesser known work by Gluck who was altogether not a good attraction as an opera composer, an unknown stage director, Volbach, and the designer also a beginner, Theo Otto. Yet the premiere was a sensation with the critics as well as the audiences. One critic wrote: "We have a Reinhardt of the opera."

You seem excited as you say that fifty-five years later.

I am trying to express how happy I was when Walther had his success in Berlin. I was ecstatic. How could I be sorry then to leave my own start of a career? Perhaps I could have such joy through him because I had not been a featured star. I had not become self-indulgent.

Did you remain in Berlin?

No. We went to Hagen Westphalia, where Walther staged an exact copy of the Berlin production. We stayed then three years in Hagen, then to Kiel, and finally to Stuttgart. There Hitler caught up with us, and we determined to leave Germany.

Hitler made no distinction between assimilated Jews and the others, did he?

Quite true. (a long pause) I had always known insecurity, financial insecurity. Little Austria lost World War I. So did Germany, but it was a bigger country, and there I was happier. But Hitler came, and everything went wrong.

What year did you actually emigrate to America?

Not until 1937. To tell a story quickly, we were in Vienna from 1933 to 1936, when Walther went to England to improve his English. A doctorate would not be enough, we knew, for employment in the future. Eventually, as you know, we got here. One year in New York with odd jobs, then to universities in the Midwest and South, and finally to Amherst— where we feel at home.

Looking way back, do you remember some roles as your favorites?

Yes, the young girls in Russian plays—Tolstoy, Gorki, Gogol. They were so much like myself. I was proud of Wendla in Wedekind's *Spring's Awakening*, a very young—a fifteen-year-old girl. One critic pointed me out as "incredibly touching." I kept that review for a long time, had it even in Texas. Maybe my favorite roles were those the critics liked.

Have you done any acting in America?

Once, soon after we arrived—remember it was during the Depression—Walther was engaged by a priest to direct plays for the Catholic Dramatic Movement in Wisconsin. The ensemble was made up of young people, more boys than girls, and they traveled around to parishes. When there was a part for an older woman, I played it. I could be Grandmother knitting in the background, but involuntarily I reacted to everything—and, of course, took the spotlight. It was much resented by the young players.

Betty Chancellor says about giving up her career as an actress to be a wife—as it turned out, a faculty wife—that somebody has to give, and she made the decision to be the one to give.

I would not put it quite that way. I was less a housewife, more a companion. Always we lived like bohemians. At first, in Germany, we had two rooms with kitchen privileges. During the first year, at Bamberg, I was learning lines by saying them aloud. When Walther came home, I had to keep quiet in those small quarters.

It sounds to me as if you made the decision to give.

I suppose it is my nature to do so. I am passive, feminine. I do not push except in an emergency, when I go against my nature. I want to say that my marriage has never been a bourgeois marriage. We have a good collaboration. Walther's artistic, uncompromising nature, his frail nerves, desperately needed a quiet place to relax and an understanding companion. Having had a glance into backstage, I was probably able to be that. And I thought this was at least as important as playing parts. Perhaps more important, as this was reality.

Was it a difficult adjustment, being a faculty wife?

No, neither in Texas nor here. In Texas I belonged to a social studies group of the University Women's Club. We met, I believe, once a month, discussing social problems. It was a congenial group, and we often ended up politicking.

I can't help wondering still about all that energy, that passion that you expanded on stage roles when you were young. What happened to it?

Feeling was strong in me, but it was transformed into the worries, the concerns of my life. Life, as it has turned out, has used me up. It might have been the theater, but because of my nature and circumstance, it was life.

———

Nature and circumstance shape our lives, and these two women, born into different cultures, thriving for a time in theaters that had in common Shakespeare and Chekhov and other classics (in the language of their audiences), have shared with me some of their thoughts about their personal selves and the conditions of their lives that made a difference to them. They both, when young, chose to act. Betty's forte was comedy, Claire's was romantic tragedy. They gave themselves wholeheartedly to the theater. They both, for reasons of the heart, for financial and domestic security, for reasons of history—"Hitler came and everything went wrong."—gave up their careers as actresses and poured their energies into lives with men of the theater, one a playwright, the other a director, both professors. Betty Chancellor and Claire Neufeld. In the future when I see them onstage in that heaven where Jan Kott imagines Ionesco endlessly attending rehearsals of *The Lesson*—the actress who played the Pupil on earth plays the role still[10]—I'd like to see Betty as Nina in *The Seagull* and Claire as Juliet. Or maybe Betty as Sabrina and Claire as Rosalind. The vitality of their recollections prompts me to cast them in many roles.

A Tribute to Denis Johnston

Only under very special circumstances have I been married to Denis Johnston, and then it was to save bus fare between Dalkey and Dublin. In 1975 I learned the trick of letting him show Betty's pass along with his, and again in 1982 I remembered the warning he gave me then: "Don't let them hear your American speech." I kept quiet, and presumably I passed for Betty. We climbed to the top of the bus, where smoking is permitted, though this year it wasn't easy for Denis to heave himself up the narrow winding steps, bus in motion, the driver negotiating curves. Listening to the passengers' speech rhythms, I sat quietly, and I looked at the profile of my companion, my dear old friend whom I have known for more than thirty years. Now his features are bleared by a patchy white beard. I remember Betty complaining about the beard he grew in 1967: "I don't want an old gaffer." She has one now, I thought, and wondered what "gaffer" really means.

Denis, when I met him in 1950, had a pencil-thin mustache. He was handsome, large, and imposing. He was six feet five inches tall. Some of the five inches have been lost to age. He entered the following in his diary in the spring of 1968.

> One evening in the summer of 1966, being present but not-at-home in the city of my birth, I was taken out to dine and brought afterwards to a temporary place of residence, where—outside, on the suburban road—in the space of fifteen seconds, I was shot into old age. Now a pacted femur has mended, but other changes have remained, chief amongst which is a noticeable limp . . . that I shall retain until the end.

To walk through Dublin streets, to go into Dublin shops with Denis Johnston at eighty! No longer securely massive, he is still impressive as he shambles handsomely down Dublin streets. And in a second-hand bookshop he introduced me to an older woman who seemed to be in charge and who greeted him with a musical "Ahhh, Mr. Johnston." When we were leaving, she threw him a challenge. "Give us more plays," she said, and he smiled in a way that suggested he just might. Also from the spring 1968 diary:

> I am out of print and long remaindered, and I
> have become a retired school teacher reduced to
> talking to myself. Probably I have always been talk-
> ing to myself, and this is the fatal flaw of my work.

The woman in the bookshop was not the only one who recognized him. A few middle-aged and older people spoke to him on the street. Looking at him with affection and admiration mingled, they called him Mr. Johnston or Denis. Back on the bus top again, we were surrounded by young toughs, some with orange punk-styled hair and American rags. The name Denis Johnston, I thought to myself, would mean nothing to them. They didn't turn to look at the old man who threw his briefcase up the steps ahead of him to gain leverage on his way to our shared seat at the very back of the bus. I noticed that anarchy was the theme of most of the graffiti on the backs of the seats and that DOWN WITH MORALITY was the most legible of the felt-tipped messages.

My companion, seemingly oblivious to his surroundings, pointed out the street where he had lived for the first twenty-five years of his life. "We used to go from house to house to dances at Christmas time," he said as his old neighborhood moved past his gaze. I recalled that Mary Manning, another transplanted Anglo-Irish writer, had written about dances where she used to encounter Denis, that "tall boy with the black hair and blue eyes." These dances "began at the ghastly hour of four o'clock and ended at half past eight because of the curfew. The Troubles were then raging." She was in her early, he in his late teens. She thought he looked like Nicholas Nickleby then.

On the bus I began to dream of the young Denis, the Judge's clever son who went to school in Dublin and in Edinburgh and then to Christ's College, Cambridge; who was a Pugsley Scholar at Harvard; who became a barrister, but who left the certainties of the law for the insecurities of the theater.

"Why the theater?" I once asked him.

With no hesitation, he replied, "I like actors and actresses. I like their gossip. They're entertaining people."

It was easy to dream on the Dalkey bus, but back at 8 Sorrento Terrace with him and Betty, I had to turn my attention to the realities of an interview with Denis Johnston, emphasis on his American years. After all, we had him for more than twenty years, counting graduate student days at Harvard and visiting lectureships out West after his retirement from New England colleges. He was in America for a crucial period in a man's life—between the ages of fifty and seventy. Now, as he looks back from the vantage point of eighty, he speaks more readily, not of the adult years but of the year when he was at Harvard (1923-1924) and the extraordinary summer of 1924 when he was an ordinary seaman.

Knowing that talk has always flowed easily between us, I was armed with only a few prepared questions. The study where we sat is a large, high-ceilinged room with a view of Killiney Bay from its tall windows. A long table in the center of the room is Denis's work table. There are piles of correspondence at one end and a small manual typewriter at the other.

Books and papers are everywhere, here and on the surfaces of smaller tables; three walls have bookcases crammed with mostly old books. There is an American corner, complete with yearbooks from the college where he spent "the most enjoyable years of my American residence," Mount Holyoke College. (How often he conjures up the names and matching anecdotes of Mount Holyoke girls of the 1950s!) The walls' icons are mostly photographs of children, grandchildren, parents, grandparents. There are maps, scenes from plays, posters. At the far end of this comfortably cluttered room is a tile fireplace, and we sat before it in armchairs on the first of two chilly spring afternoons—to talk about America.

My first question, "If you could capture on film scenes that you witnessed in America, what would they be?," received an immediate response: "Dances in Boston during Prohibition and my trip to Tampico."

At Harvard, Denis learned law by the case system, a new experience for him. For Felix Frankfurter's seminar, he wrote a paper, "The Implementation of the Anglo-Irish Treaty." At Widener Library he read indiscriminately and with joy. He read and rejected Freud: "It's no sort of subject to dabble in and one best left alone altogether, I guess," according to his January 15, 1924 diary entry.

Like most students, he studied during the week, and on weekends, he played. What he remembers especially about that year are the plays he saw on Beacon Hill—his interest in theater began with these amateur groups and their "photographic realism"; touch football even in winter, with the team half girls, half boys; reading Shaw for the first time at the Harvard Union and having his eyes opened by the prefaces, especially the preface to *Androcles and the Lion*. And, oh yes, those dances. "It was Prohibition. So there were always bottles." And there were new customs for the visiting Irishman to learn.

"A half dozen of us at the Harvard Law School were pursued, invited out a lot in Cambridge and Boston. One high society ball I remember was at the Copley Plaza." He sits lost in memories of the occasion, elbows on the arms of his chair, his fingertips touching beneath his beard in a characteristic gesture of contemplation. "It was highly organized. I arrived at nine o'clock, the time announced, but there was no sign of life until about ten. I think I read a book while I waited. There was a reception line, and I did meet the girl whose party it was. There were ushers who wore flowers. They could introduce you, cut in for you, and then you danced until someone cut in on you. Then back to the stag line. A stag line, men in a gang in the middle of the floor, was a new thing to me. Each time you danced with someone you had never met before. Free and easy American hospitality. I liked it. Some fellows I knew were in the band. They danced when they weren't playing. Actually there were two bands. The music never stopped. A so-called supper was served, and we opened the sandwiches to see what was inside." His January 15, 1924 diary entry continues:

> I could have as nice a time as I liked or as rotten a one according to my own gumption. I had to learn to seize an usher and point out a girl I fancied. He's entitled to cut in, as an usher, and to introduce the girl to her new partner . . . Two large bands, about a hundred couples: "A Small Dance—to meet the Misses Winslow"

But after the lectures, the libraries, the theaters, the dances, the picnics, the kissing and popular songs, what he remem-

bers most vividly in his diaries and remembers most vividly
in his darkening study is a trip by tanker from New York,
down the east coast, past the Florida Keys, through the Gulf
of Mexico to Tampico and, after a leave, on to New Orleans.
On January 19, 1924, he wrote in the diary:

> At a tea party I met a first-year man named
> Anthony who says he worked his way round to Los
> Angeles on an oil tanker last summer. It's not hard
> to arrange. I wonder if it could be done. It's rather
> an idea.

Today he says, "All college boys took such trips in summer."
(A statement I doubt, but I let it stand.) And he remembers
that he earned $47.50 a month.

One incident comes back clearly, a confrontation with a
fellow crew member, a Norwegian. As Denis remembers it,
they were about to go on leave in Tampico and Denis was
washing out his shirt when a big guy, drunk, wanted to fight.
Denis almost threw him overboard; he had to be rescued by
the rest of the crew. "I made rather a mess of him," he says
proudly even at this late date. "When I had to be fierce I was.
The guy came back sober and wanted to fight, but I said I
had just been protecting myself. I added that I'd fight him in
New Orleans. To my surprise, he was not interested in a fight
when we got to New Orleans."

Needless to say, there was no time for diary keeping on a
tanker, but a year later, back in Dublin, Denis recorded the
experience.

> My tanker—*S. M. Spaulding* . . . the sweating
> cook, the blasting pump man, and the somewhat
> philosophic quartermaster—and me asleep on the
> shot-silk sea of the Florida Keys. Hell down in the
> tanks, bucketing, bucketing, bucketing—Tampico

and its railway track—the smack of my bare fists on Norsker flesh that Sunday night, when I found myself in a new and rather surprising phase. The Gulf and its sweating sun . . . and New Orleans—the Woman City of the South—the brown Mississippi.

The crew of the *S. M. Spaulding* had nicknames worthy of characters in an early O'Neill play, names like Dutchy, Slim, and Scotty. An incident in Tampico had Scotty in a leading role. "We didn't realize at first that the shanties in Tampico were whorehouses. Girls just sat out front. Scotty went inside with one of them, and the rest of us waited. He came out in half an hour, which surprised me when I learned what he was doing. I thought it took all night."

From New Orleans, where they were paid, Denis went by boat and train to Washington, D. C., and on to New York City. "I wanted to see the Mississippi Valley. It was as romantic as the Danube. I took a boat—it was cheap—the better to see the river. An immigration officer came aboard and ticked us off on a list. There I was in my cut-down sea boots, and I still had a black eye. 'Irishman,' he said. 'I'm not surprised.'" To the Norwegian, who was also present and also looking the worse for wear, Denis reports that the officer said, "You've had a rough crossing."

A girlfriend from Cambridge brought him a change of clothes when she met him in Washington, and on they went to New York, where he had a last wild week of partying in the Village, visiting Harlem (this was, after all, the twenties), enjoying what he later called "careless, untrammeled Bohemianism." To this day he remembers "the friendliness of people. Fights, yes. But no subsequent nastiness. Everyone on the same social level." One wonders what his parents made of him when they met him at Derry. "I came back to Dublin," he says, "a changed man."

When I met Denis Johnston in 1950, I was a graduate
student, studying theater with Hallie Flanagan Davis at
Smith College. He was beginning his round-robin career in
the Connecticut Valley, a career that meant first teaching at
Amherst College (spelling his admirer and astute early critic
Curtis Canfield), then at Mount Holyoke, at Smith, back to
Amherst briefly, to the University of Massachusetts for a
seminar and occasional lecture. But by 1950 he was already a
distinguished playwright, one whom Una Ellis-Fermor had
referred to as early as 1939 as "a dramatist of originality and
versatility whose work has been received with interest in
Ireland, England, and America."[10] In 1982, then—neglecting
the barrister, war correspondent, film and television director, whose careers, after all, did not belong to America, and
instead fastening on the commercial man of the theater that
preceded the academic—I decided to frame my next question
to move us along to the playwright.

"What was your first play on Broadway?" I asked. "What
was the experience like for you?" "*The Moon in the Yellow
River* was the only one on Broadway," he answered. "*The Old
Lady Says 'No'!* doesn't count because the Gate brought it to
New York." (It was in the Dublin Gate's repertory during its
Broadway engagement in 1948.) Then the phone rang in the
hall, and Denis excused himself to answer it. I could hear,
even with the door closed, that someone was inviting him to
do a reading, and he was accepting. He hung up the phone
and then, instead of returning, seemed to go upstairs. Perhaps our first session was over.

I moved to a window and looked out at the gray waters of
Killiney Bay and the Sugar Loaf mountains beyond. (We'd
call them hills at home.) Rain was spitting at the glass. The

peat fire was warm at my back. Ireland. What a magnet! During the years Denis had spent away from Ireland, he was never in exile except in a part-time sense. His was the interrupted exile of an academic. Each summer he came home from America to Ireland. Now he is home, as we say, for good. "I'm back with my Betty," he wrote me a few years ago, "staring at the short but vicious breakers of the Irish Sea."

My musing was interrupted by Denis's return to the study. In his hand he had what looked like a ledger and what turned out to be one of his diaries. After the phone call he had gone to the landing of the Georgian staircase where, in a heavy green box—a Spanish sea chest with a complicated system of locks in its cover—he keeps the many notebooks where he has been scribbling his response to life for nearly sixty years. What he proceeded to share with me was the entry for December 31, 1931, the story of his visit to the Theater Guild when they were producing *The Moon in the Yellow River*, which had had its premiere at the Dublin Gate Theater that spring. (It opened in Philadelphia on February 15 and in New York on February 29, 1932.) He talked a bit about the Theater Guild experience and then handed me the precious diary, a record kept in the neat scrawl of his youth, with here and there the occasional emendations of the older man made in an almost illegible hand. "The Past is better of a re-write," he wrote in his seventies at the bottom of a page written in his twenties, "as is this book."

When the Theater Guild invited the young author to attend some production meetings in New York that December, he accepted with pleasure—in part, no doubt, because he could combine the visit with one to his then wife, Shelah Richards, who was appearing in Cincinnati, with the touring Abbey Theater company. (Denis Johnston had a gift for combining business and pleasure.) So he went to Cincinnati for Christmas, then on to New York where he saw O'Neill's *Mourning Becomes Electra*, also a Theater Guild production, and attended interminable meetings about his own play. . . .

As the afternoon wore on and our time ran out, I was beginning to realize that Denis Johnston deserves either much more than I am prepared to write about him or else the kind of succinct legend accompanying a sketch of Samuel Beckett on a postcard I bought in Dublin: "Samuel Beckett was educated at Miss Elsner's Kindergarten Academy in Stillorgan and at Trinity College Dublin where he achieved renown as a cricketer. Later migrated to Paris where he became acquainted with penman James Joyce." Anything in between will be inadequate.

This anecdotal man, my old friend Denis, would not be confined to the traditional format of an interview. I knew that from the beginning but also knew I'd forget to ask key questions if I didn't set aside a couple of blocks of time. In between, however, embroidering on our accounts of events we had shared with each other years before, he and Betty and I randomly told each other stories. Revisionist anecdotes are allowed between us. We ask questions in a way to encourage new details. (I was long ago prepared for this game by a saga-spinning grandmother who taught me that anything goes if it "makes a good story.") And so, as we walked, as we ate meals, we told each other truths we had agreed upon, tempered truths concerning our shared past.

We can almost call out the stories by number. There's the Wystan Auden story—when he walked, vaudeville style, into the hall closet in South Hadley, thinking he was making an exit to the outdoors. There are other Auden stories, but this one will serve. ("Wystan," I remember Betty saying once, "looks like a tailor's dummy that has been left out in the rain.") Or the time Denis saw Joan Crawford on television and remarked drily, "O'Flaherty said she has the soul of a rat." And the time Franz Werfel's sister—we always called her Madame Rieser, though I suppose she had a first name—came to Highfield, the summer theater on Cape Cod where we were employed in 1950, to bring a script to Denis. I believe she wanted help with re-writes. She was a Sarah Bernhardt look-alike who arrived in a white touring car driven by a black chauffeur. For the week or so that she stayed with us (unbidden and largely ignored), she wore a white pantsuit and a white yachting cap for all occasions. And there was the evening in 1958 when I went with Denis to Cambridge for the opening of his play *The Scythe and the Sunset*, produced by the Poets Theater on a small stage at one end of what seemed once to have been an artist's studio. We were so late that we had to sit at the very back of the tightly packed room, on the edge of an old slate sink—an easier job for Denis at his height than for me at mine; at least his feet touched the floor. By now I think the water faucet dripped all the way through the play. And there was the lovely time that Micheal MacLiammóir visited the Johnstons in Northampton, when he was touring *The Importance of Being Oscar*, his one-man show about Oscar Wilde. I went with Denis to see him in Springfield. (Auden had been a brilliant Lady Bracknell at the Johnston's dinner table years before, but he couldn't hold a candle to MacLiammóir.) After the show we were invited to an Irish-American club, where Denis and I sat on wooden folding chairs waiting for the guest of honor (who was the only one in our party to get any of the refreshments being served). Just as well, for when we got back to Northampton, Betty served us Chinese food at midnight. Then the real stories began, theater stories featuring Betty Chancellor and Michael MacLiammóir. In that company, I was content to listen, though of course I was adding to my own repertoire.

My second "interview" was scheduled for the last day of my visit, for the afternoon before the evening when Denis was invited to do a reading at an Irish Theater Company benefit in Dublin. When I expressed the worry that this might be too much activity for him in one day, he assured me he would be fine. Remembering his catnaps, I believed him. Denis has always been able to escape into a quiet snooze, seated in an armchair, on a bus, even at dinner. Anyone who thinks this habit has come on him with age hasn't known him for very long.

Waiting in the study alone, I thought of how much more of America the Johnstons have seen than I have seen of their Ireland. I now know this little corner, Dublin and Dalkey, pretty well. I know how to get to Trinity College Library, where to find the best coffee in Dublin (at Bewley's, of course), and how to manage the bus between city and suburb. I know a few shops in each place. I have seen Hugh Leonard's house— *Da*'s author had come back to his hometown, too—quiet and closed in the mornings because he writes at night, cars coming and going in the afternoons. I've bought meat and cheese in Dalkey, but I've never eaten in a restaurant. (Denis says one of them once had the distinction of closing for lunch.) Mostly I will remember the winding streets that converge unexpectedly and the sudden beauty of Killiney Bay.

Once Betty told me about her arrival in America. She landed in Boston at night and was whisked off to nearby Concord. When she awoke in that New England town, she told me, she felt right at home, for she had grown up reading Louisa May Alcott! I thought of that sweet beginning when she wrote me many years later from California, "Sacramento is a good-looking town. It has two murders a day."

In danger of more general reminiscing, I began to prepare myself for Denis's arrival by thinking about his teaching. I never had a formal course with him, but I learned much from being directed by him. Any student of theater knows that the best learning can take place in rehearsal periods. As a director, with good humor and finesse, he effortlessly and clearly gave us instructions. I learned timing for farce from Denis Johnston. (Well, from him and the Marx brothers.) He showed me how all the little comic bits add up to significant moments in farce. As a director he was a master of comic timing. (As a performer, Betty takes the prize.) I realize, too, that the plays he brought to our stages were important; we might have missed them otherwise. In a period when too many colleges were producing warmed-over Broadway shows, he directed plays by Shaw, Ibsen, Strindberg, Synge, Pirandello, Benavente—who of us had ever heard of Jacinto Benavente?—and even a dramatization of James Joyce's *Finnegan's Wake* (how it delighted him when some members of the audience walked out on that one, proving to him that he had accomplished the intended shock). Of course, his students didn't know then, except through program notes, who this man Denis Johnston was before he came to them. Like all young people, they thought the present was everything, and so he was theirs alone.

So immersed was I in the past that the appearance of Denis in the doorway of the study startled me. He was wearing not his customary wool jacket (it had been rained on that morning) but his navy blue Cambridge blazer. His good looks were enhanced by the dark jacket. He stood waiting to be asked into his own study, no doubt because I showed my obvious preoccupation with something other than the moment at hand.

Once we were settled in our armchairs, I asked him about teaching. He claims never to have regretted his decision to live in the academic, not the professional theater world. He hints that his original decision to move in that direction had something to do with his observing the production of *The Old Lady Says "No"*! when the Dublin Gate brought it to Broadway in 1948. "The Gate company was casual," he says. "But the chorus members, New York actors, were earnestly fighting for their lives. Happily, my experience in America was mostly with academic theater." This in answer to my asking if he had known Lillian Hellman or S. N. Behrman, both of whom were doing interesting things on Broadway in the thirties and forties. Foolishly, I forgot to ask him about O'Neill. "No. I don't believe I met them." Then on to the subject of teaching.

I got him to agree with V. S. Pritchett, another octogenarian, who said in a *New York Times* interview two years ago: "I like teaching because it wakes me up and teaches me."

"I especially liked teaching the girls," Denis says.

"And the boys?"

"They were not so advanced, so challenging—at least not in the fifties. By the time I was teaching out West, by the mid sixties, the boys had caught up a bit."

The course that remains in his memory as his favorite was a Yeats course he taught at Mount Holyoke. "Yes, I liked that Anglo-Irish course very much." I remarked that I always have to remember to look him up in both Irish and Anglo-Irish reference books. "When I'm called Anglo-Irish, what's really meant is that I'm Protestant, Protestant Irish." This observation leads him to tell me that the Johnstons were driven out of Scotland. "I like genealogy; families go up and down like ball teams. My family nearly always picked the wrong side."

Today, I reminded him, in whichever reference book I consult, I find him called the major Irish playwright since O'Casey. *The 1979 Dictionary of Irish Literature* claims that "he has been the most intelligent and, with Samuel Beckett, the most daring Irish playwright of his time."

"Oh, yes," he says. "My plays were denounced originally. Now some of the same ones who denounced them are coming back with praise—coming back loving what they seemed to despise." I find it impossible to know whether he was more hurt then than he is delighted now. His cynicism seems to be cheerful.

I resume my questioning: "Have you moved from being an 'unknown gurrier' to being a 'distinguished old buff'?" He recognizes my reference to Dublinisms used by him on past public occasions, though only in the first instance about himself. In 1977 when he received a £1000 award from the Allied Irish Banks for "excellence in creative writing," he was quoted as declaring:

I am the Unknown Gurrier of Irish letters, in the sense that no copy of my works is to be found in the Dublin bookshops. Either they are out of print or the two copies they had last year have disappeared, even when the bookseller is the publisher, so transatlantic writers of theses who wish to find out how to spell my name have to call and stay in the house unless they have the money to go to Coleraine where most of my detritus can be found.

When I first read the newspaper account—this is only part of a paragraph from a five-column, quarter-page story—sent me by his best agent, Betty, I asked a student of Irish literature, one of those "transatlantic writers of theses," for a definition of gurrier. "A gurrier," I was told, "is Dublin slang for a gutter character on the make." Denis says it means "a slum dweller, and the slum is a mental slum." And what is a buff? That's someone who is "not socially acceptable, a cod trying to live on a past reputation."

I apologized for using the term buff in my question. I had fallen for his use of it on an earlier occasion—he was referring to Yeats, Beckett, and Joyce at a Canadian Irish studies meeting—completely missing his irony. Mea culpa. I realized I had better ask about the term cod, even though I knew I was going off the track of my interview. "A cod is someone who has pretensions to what he doesn't deserve. He mentions places he hasn't been." Denis here does a lilting imitation of a cod's speech. "He says he's been to Paris to see Jimmy Joyce—had a wonderful evening with Jimmy Joyce." Denis leans toward me to say emphatically, "It must be Jimmy. A cod makes his listeners feel inferior, left out." Then I remembered reading the word "codology" in Hugh Leonard's autobiography, *Home Before Night*. "Codology," Denis told me, "is talking rubbish you hope will be believed." I wondered about other words I have missed in Irish stories and remembered Denis saying that he got to know the American language early and rather easily. "Everybody translates the language for you in America. You soon know what's guff."

"Who are the authors you have read and still read for pleasure?" I asked, getting in my final question.

"As you know, Shaw opened my eyes when I was a young man. You could say that first I became a Shavian; then I became myself. To the end I loved Shaw." Here a digression about his having lunch with Shaw—"When I left, I realized that he had never mentioned my plays, only his own."—and the old man's "implied encouragement" of Denis's early stage and television career. I asked if he reads Beckett. I remembered him once saying that *Waiting for Godot* is the perfect expression of the fifties. "Oh, yes. I like *Godot* and *Krapp* especially." (Krapp has his tapes, and Johnston has his diaries, I thought.) He went in search of a Beckett book he has been reading. "Must be fair to Beckett," he muttered. The book turned out to be one I had never seen, *How It Is* (1964). Some of the passages are underlined, others starred. "Beckett is climbing on Joyce," he said. "Joyce is the beginning. *Juno* is a nice piece of work, but O'Casey wrote rubbish in his later years. Beckett is exploiting his earlier plays now, but he still interests me." The answer to my question, then, is that Denis mostly reads and re-reads what he calls the "brilliant original Irish writers." As he says, "I know what they are talking about."

He had a nice Beckett anecdote for me. "I never spoke to him that I remember," says Denis. "But one night we were both at the Campbells' in a fairly large group, and Beckett said nothing all evening, just sat staring silently into the fire. At that time he lived at Fox Rock, and at the end of the evening a man who also lived there asked him for a ride. 'May I have a ride?' the man asked. 'No' was all Beckett answered."

During the course of the afternoon Denis invited me to join him that evening for the Irish Theater Company benefit in Dublin. The Irish *Times* had announced the day before that he would read from *The Old Lady Says "No"*! He had never agreed to that, he says, but plans instead to read a bit of *Nine Rivers from Jordan*. Between our session and dinner I see him walking about the house with the book in hand, putting it down, picking it up, reading in it—not rehearsing, just planning which paragraphs to read and perhaps timing them.

It seemed extraordinary to me but not to Denis and Betty that the cab calling for us was to arrive at ten p.m. I realized later that it was to allow theater folks to come in after their shows. Denis and I were ready at 9:30. I was substituting for Betty because a recent fall had kept her from getting about without a stick; the cold, rainy night was not for her. Denis did seem nervous. The Irish Theater Company, which had been in existence only since 1974, had recently produced his play *The Scythe and the Sunset.* "I owe them one," he says, and I can't help wondering if he doesn't owe himself an occasion. He needs to be "on stage" now and then. We all do if we have ever been there and felt the exhilaration of applause.

Seeing Denis standing near the front door, his coat on, his book under his arm, with a look of apprehension on his face, Betty says, "Someone said of Denis once that he 'stood in the doorway looking like a sullen archangel.'" Remembering the line, he smiles, and I feel sure Betty is citing it accurately.

The cab arrived at ten o'clock, and the driver made good time, getting us to Powerscourt Townhouse Centre for an event advertised as "Some Words and Music" not long after its scheduled beginning at 10:30 p.m. This time, unlike the times on the bus, I was not taken for Denis's wife but for his manager. It would have delighted him if I could have "gone along with the gag," but I was much too intimidated by the show's producers. A temporary stage had been built across the courtyard of the elegant Dublin shopping center, and we were seated at a table near it on the upper level or balcony, in a draft. Before Denis's reading there was music, a lot of music: a jazz quartet, followed by a brass ensemble, followed by a string quartet. The crowd below in the courtyard was very young and growing noisy as time passed. Those at tables on our level, for no reason that I could tell—they had all paid "IR £2.00 (to include wine)" according to the program—looked older, more prosperous than the ones downstairs.

When Denis and I walked over to a cappuccino stand across the courtyard between numbers, several people shook his hand and some asked him to autograph their programs. He seemed delighted by the general attention, but it was one young actor who most pleased him that night. He came by our table and introduced himself to Denis as the actor who had played Palliser in the recent production of *Scythe*. "I had a mustache then," he said, and Denis's face lit up in recognition of him. They spoke of the production, and the actor said, "If some members of the audience didn't understand the play, Mr. Johnston, that wasn't your fault." Then he added, "And it wasn't my fault either." They shook hands warmly in acknowledgement of their collaboration, one at eighty and the other at maybe twenty-five. The actor left, inviting the playwright to come see him in *Amadeus*. "I'll try. I'll surely try," said Denis. And I wished I were in a position to ask the young man to recite Palliser's exit line: "Winter gives back the roses to the frost-filled earth." Somehow it would have been a perfect gift from boy to man, from collaborators to audience. It was not, however, that kind of evening.

Just as Denis and I were beginning to look at each other with mutual fear that he might never get on stage, that we were doomed to listen to "one more encore" for eternity, the master of ceremonies came by to say, "You're next, Mr. Johnston." By now it was after midnight. The noise and smoke levels were high. Very wisely, the emcee said to Denis, "Register your presence, Mr. Johnston. Register your presence." That's all the cue Denis needed. With a sense of timing learned from more than fifty years in the theater, he rose, coat over his shoulders, and moved slowly but certainly into the spotlight. When the light hit his white hair, and he raised a hand in greeting, they stood to cheer him. He read only a few poetic lines from his book and walked back to sustained applause. He had registered his presence.

Soon after, he ordered a cab, and we left. A woman was singing cabaret songs from Brecht-Weill shows when we made our exit. She was good, but she was asserting her presence.

It was two a.m. when Denis and I arrived at 8 Sorrento Terrace. We sat in the kitchen for a while, drinking Irish whiskey and hot water and rehearsing the events of the "evening." Then we drifted into talk of old age, of his father and grandfather. (He had marked Beckett's line: "Scraps of an ancient voice in me not mine.") He told me that his father didn't wake him to see Halley's Comet in 1910. "He told me I could see it next time." Next time will be late 1985 or early 1986. "I am determined to live that long—but no longer," he declared. "I don't want to live to be in the region of refuse." Who does, Denis? Who does?

Before I went to sleep that morning I looked at the last chapter of *Nine Rivers From Jordan*, the controversial chapter in which Denis kills himself off in his prime. He writes:

Death is not necessarily a deplorable end. It comes in any event, and having graduated, I shall be taken much more seriously. I may be misquoted but never happily contradicted. I am the Dead— dead in my prime . . . .

I am spared the pot belly and the gobs, the pasty flesh, and the reek of old age . . . .

I shall not live to be a burden and an offense to

all my dear ones or to disappoint my children with
the inevitable Noes of parenthood. I shall not live
to be a Bore in all the Clubs, and the worst of all
bores—the fellow with something on his mind.

These words were written thirty years ago. How easy it
is to praise death when one's life is nowhere near its amen.
Today, of course, he wants a few more years. He'd like to go
out by the light of Halley's Comet.

At the airport on the day of my departure, I noticed that
Denis's shoes were untied. There was nothing unusual about
that. "Tie your laces, Denis," Betty had said that morning.
"You put the heart across me with those laces." But here he
was, laces still undone. He insisted on carrying bags, and
when they were deposited at the counter, he stood looking
at me as if to say something more, but all that came out was
"Goodbye." We kissed, and I said, "See you, Denis." We
moved away from each other, and then each turned back
for one more look. He raised his fingers to his forehead in a
salute. I blew him a kiss. When I saw him walk away, hands
clasped behind his back, I thought, "You put the heart across
me, Denis Johnston."

More about Betty Chancellor, Claire Neufeld, and Denis Johnston

Betty Chancellor (1910-1984) was always Betty Johnston to me, because I didn't meet her until 1950. Her husband Denis was directing plays in the summer of 1950 at Highfield Theater in Falmouth, Massachusetts. I was a member of the acting company. Betty was busy as the mother of two young boys, though she did find time to play a few small roles. Her professional career in the theater had been principally in the forties. She acted at the Dublin Gate Theater, which was in the competent hands of Micheal MacLiammóir and Hilton Edwards. MacLiammóir's *All for Hecuba* (1946) is an important source for stories about Betty Chancellor and Denis Johnston.

Claire Neufeld (1895-1993) had a brief career in the professional theater in Austria and Germany before World War II. She has left fewer traces than the companion I have given her in "Two Actresses." A beautiful portrait of Claire is in private hands. She and her beloved husband Walther are buried in Amherst's West Cemetery, not far from Emily Dickinson's grave. Only a few of us take the short walk to acknowledge Claire and Walther.

Denis Johnston (1901-1984) was a practicing barrister in London and Dublin, a playwright and a director for stage and television, a war correspondent and a professor. He came to the United States in 1950 to be a visiting professor at Amherst College. All the colleges in the area—Smith College, Mount Holyoke College, and the University of Massachusetts—claimed him over the next twenty years. After that, he was a visiting professor in Iowa, New York, and California. All the while, his plays were being performed here and abroad. Anyone wanting to get to know Johnston should be encouraged to read his *Nine Rivers From Jordan* (1953), an unconventional war chronicle that allows the reader to join the writer in his search for himself.

Notes

[1]Erving Goffman, *The Presentation of Self in Everyday Life* (New York: Anchor Books, 1959), p. 18.

[2]Micheal MacLiammóir, *All for Hecuba: An Irish Autobiography* (London: Methuen & Co., 1946), pp. 273-274.

[3]According to Betty, she arrived at the Dublin Gate in 1928.

[4]MacLiammóir, p. 109.

[5]Meriel Moor. She and Coralie Carmichael and Betty Chancellor shared leading roles at the Dublin Gate.

[6]Shelah Richards, Denis Johnston's first wife. She too was an actress, and mother of Jennifer and Michael. Betty's children are Jeremy and Rory.

[7]Flora Ludington, Mount Holyoke Librarian.

[8]MacLiammóir, p. 322.

[9]On another occasion, when I commented to Walther on what vital gestures he and Claire both use in their conversations (both are in their eighties), he said: "There are those with bent backs and hands arthritic who have vital gestures in their heads. They can't express them. We are so far fortunate."

[10]Jan Kott, *Theater Notebook: 1947-1967* (New York: Doubleday & Co., 1968) p. 219

Syllables and Sounds

Doris Abramson reads her poetry, a compact disc

from *Time Will Tell*, copyright 2007 by Doris Abramson

from *It's Time*, copyright 1998 and 2007 by Doris Abramson